BRITAIN IN OLD PHOTOGRAPHS

PRESTWICH

HELEN CALLAGHAN

ALAN SUTTON PUBLISHING LIMITED

Alan Sutton Publishing Limited
Phoenix Mill · Far Thrupp · Stroud
Gloucestershire · GL5 2BU

First published 1996

Copyright © Helen Callaghan, 1996

Cover photographs: *front*; Heaton Park Bazaar,
c. 1910; *back*; sheep being driven into
Harrison's, a butcher's shop with its own
slaughterhouse, on the corner of Church Lane
and Bury New Road, *c.* 1906.

British Library Cataloguing in Publication Data
A catalogue record for this book is available from the
British Library.

ISBN 0-7509-1173-5

Typeset in 10/12 Perpetua.
Typesetting and origination by
Alan Sutton Publishing Limited.
Printed in Great Britain by
Ebenezer Baylis, Worcester.

CONTENTS

An early photograph of Benjamin Carver of Polefield House, Justice of the Peace, alderman of the county, and dedicatee of *The Annals of Prestwich*, published 1902.

INTRODUCTION

The name 'Prestwich' is commonly held to mean 'the Priest's village', or 'the Priest's retreat', and is believed to indicate that Prestwich has been occupied since Saxon times.

Local archaeologists insist that Prestwich has been occupied for much longer than that, and certainly it was known to the Romans. They established a fort at Rainsough that overlooked the Irwell valley and Manchester. Roman pottery has been found at Rainsough, and early coins discovered by the side of Bury New Road.

The earliest reference to the village was in 1200, when Thomas, Rector of Prestwich, was attested a grant of half of Denton by Matthew de Reddish. This reference appears in the Wilton deeds. Certainly Prestwich is not mentioned in the Domesday Book (1080–6), though there is a mention of a Robert de Prestwich, who in 1193 was fined four marks for supporting a rebellion against Richard I.

The village's great antiquity and rich parish – St Mary's parish once extended as far as Oldham – has left a wealth of historical and archaeological evidence, especially in the church. The tower of St Mary's was built in 1500 by the Earl of Derby, who was granted much of the local estate after the Wars of the Roses. Chantry chapels (small chapels where a single priest was hired to pray continuously for a dead person's soul) were built and still remain. Kersal Cell and the Deyne (the old rectory) were raised at about this time.

This prosperity continued for hundreds of years, despite the vagaries of the Civil War and the plague, but the Industrial Revolution set in motion a chain of events that was to change the character of Prestwich for ever.

Wealthy industrialists, using the resources of the Irwell and the local environment and looking about for semi-rural retreats within striking distance of the industrial hub of Manchester, settled eagerly on Prestwich. Most of the palatial homes they built or bought from landed gentry have sadly disappeared or fallen into decay, but some, like Philips Park Hall and Bent Hall, survive to testify to the standard of living enjoyed by these factory owners in the boom years of the last century.

However, the process of urbanization continued long after the gentry had disappeared. Increasingly, more and more green space was used to build housing for the growing population of Manchester, and the residents of a hundred years ago would now have some difficulty in recognizing the village. Some beauty spots remain, though, such as Prestwich Clough and Mere Clough, currently being developed in the Red Rose Forest Scheme, and the grounds of Heaton Park, which are still open to all. But on the whole, the construction of the M62 motorway merely put the top hat on the rising urbanization of the village. Matters were not helped by the amalgamation of Prestwich council with Bury in 1972, as a consequence of the Local Government Act.

It is the latest round of these changes, such as the closure of Prestwich Hospital to a great extent, and accompanying new developments, that have prompted this author's desire to try to present as much material as possible from this vanishing Prestwich, before it is gone for ever. My aim in compiling this book is not to advance the field of Prestwich scholarship to any great degree (Prestwich is full of committed local antiquarians who could perform such a task with infinitely more aplomb than I) but merely to present these photographs, some never seen before, and, in doing so, to raise awareness of the venerable history and distinctive character of this our village.

CHURCH AND CLOUGH

St Mary's parish church, c. 1919.

St Mary's church before extensions, 1880s. Founded in the thirteenth century, on an ancient religious site, the parish of St Mary's once extended as far as Oldham. The tower was built in 1500 by the Earl of Derby, when the Pilkington estates were granted to him after the Wars of the Roses. The Victorian era saw more building and the great east window, erected in honour of Mary Margaret, Countess of Wilton, was put into place. In later building work (1887–9) the chancel was extended and the window replaced in the new east wall.

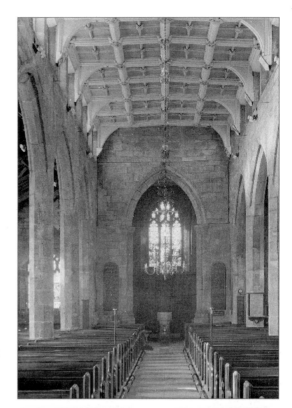

The nave of St Mary's. The view faces the font and tower. These photographs were taken after 1974, when the fine ceilings had been rediscovered after restoration work. (BLS)

St Mary's interior. These arches are all that remain of the original Norman church. (BLS)

St Mary's interior, 1926. The north and south galleries, built in the eighteenth century, were demolished in 1959. In times past, families would pay for seats in the church, and the galleries probably helped raise revenue. (BLS)

Brooks Monument. The marble tomb monument was displayed at the Great Exhibition in 1851 before being erected in the churchyard. John Brooks, industrialist, and his wife Alice are interred beneath.

Pre-Second World War graveyard. During the war, all the railings lining the graves were taken down and used as scrap for armaments.

St Mary's church and Church Inn, *c.* 1919. The Church Inn dates back to the seventeenth century, and there may well have been an inn on this site since the 1400s.

Approach to Prestwich Clough. In the 1930s the land on the left was bought by the parish and is now part of the graveyard.

Early view of St Mary's from Rainsough, *c.* 1910.

Lowther Road, *c*. 1900. The line of trees crossing the road marks the deep valley that is Prestwich Clough. The stream at the bottom flows into the River Irwell. The Clough has been a local beauty spot and of interest to naturalists for over a hundred years.

The bandstand in Prestwich Clough, *c.* 1915. The Clough was dedicated to public use in 1906.

Refreshment rooms, Prestwich Clough. The Clough was a popular place for picnics and Sunday walks, and still serves that function to this day, though the refreshment rooms are long gone.

Sunday strollers near the bandstand, *c.* 1910. The oak in the centre is still going strong, though the 'rustic' latticework seating surrounding it has vanished.

The 'rustic' bridge in Prestwich Clough, 1900s.

Prestwich Clough with strollers, from a hand-coloured postcard, *c.* 1910.

Asylum, or Mere Clough, 1920s. This deep cleft, once a packhorse trail, ran parallel to Prestwich Clough on the other side of the asylum, before joining it at Drinkwater. It is unchanged today.

STREETS

Bury New Road, 1920s. This road was first built in the 1820s, following the line of a footpath from Prestwich to Manchester, which may itself have followed the line of the old Roman road. Previously traffic to Manchester went via Bury Old Road.

Bury New Road, Prestwich, *c.* 1916. The shops on the left were demolished to make way for Tower buildings, site of Prestwich Co-op.

Boys playing in Bury New Road, 1920s.

Horse and cart on Bury New Road, 1900s.

Prestwich village at the turn of the century. (BLS)

Prestwich village, 1920s. The clock tower belongs to the National School. The old Labour Exchange is on the far right.

The corner of Bury New Road and Clarks Hill, from a hand-coloured postcard.

Bury New Road, 1930s. Tram no. 8 ran to Eccles Green. The Methodist church is on the left. Built in 1877, it was designed by John Lowe. It had extensive schools, and parts of these buildings still survive.

Longfield, 1960s. Before the present Longfield Centre was built, a street of terraced cottages connected Bury New Road to the railway station. They were knocked down in 1965. (BLS)

Bury Old Road, 1924. Until Bury New Road was built in the 1820s, this was the main route to Manchester.

A view of Gardner Road, a rather elegant street at this time, 1900s.

Two cottages owned by a Mr Hilton, on Longfield, 1889. The next year he sold them to the postal service, who built a post office on the site. This post office is now Barclays Bank on Bury New Road. (BLS)

Rectory Lane with 'the Dingle' on the left. Previously Prestwich Clough extended all the way to Rectory Lane, before St Mary's Playing Fields were created by draining and levelling the Dingle in 1931.

An illustration from the 'Prestwich Guide Calendar' showing Rectory Lane. (BLS)

Deyne Avenue, 1920. At the top is the site of The Deyne – the old rectory built in 1485. The new rectory was built on Church Lane in 1923. (BLS)

Ramsbottom Row, a row of poor cottages in Prestwich village – long since demolished.

Kersley cottages on Hodge Lane. The little girl playing outside one of them grew up to be one Mrs Townsend. (BLS)

Kersley cottages in the early years of this century. Polefield library now occupies this site; the cottages were demolished in 1937. (BLS)

Hodge Lane, leading to Polefield Hall. (BLS)

Rainsough Brow. The big building on the far right is the Prestwich workhouse, which closed in 1869. It was sold at auction in 1874, and has now been demolished.

Wesleyan chapel, Rainsough, *c.* 1890. The chapel was built in 1874.

Thatched cottage, Rainsough, *c.* 1890. The last thatched building in the area was Philip's Park Lodge, which stood in a ruinous state until 1969, when it was demolished to make way for the motorway.

Hartswell flooded, 1900s. These poor cottages were built at the bottom of Rainsough Brow, near the banks of the Irwell at Drinkwater. Flooding was a constant danger.

Hartswell flooded, 1900s. These cottages were eventually evacuated and demolished in 1937. They were not replaced.

Bury Old Road, with St Margaret's School on the left. The tram, a no. 66, is travelling to Monton.

Besses-o'-th'-Barn tollgate, 1860s. The tollgate was dismantled in 1880. (BLS)

HEATON PARK

Postcard view of Heaton Park Grand Lodge, c. 1905. Heaton Park was the seat of the Earls of Wilton and their ancestors, the Holland family, for 560 years. It was sold to the Manchester Corporation for £230,000 in 1902 and opened to the public.

Heaton Park newsagent, 1890s. The station is on the far right. (BLS)

Gates to Heaton Park grounds, with a view of the station, 1930s.

A very early postcard of Grand Lodge and grounds, *c.* 1910. (BLS)

Tame deer and gamekeeper, *c.* 1880.

Inspection of the 17th Service battalion (2nd Pals) in Heaton Park. Heaton Park was used as a transit camp during both world wars. (BLS)

Earl of Wilton's coach, 1880s. The third Earl of Wilton, Arthur Edward Holland Grey, inherited the title on the death of his father in 1882. He held it for only three years, dying in 1885, and it passed on to his brother, Seymour John Grey Egerton. (BLS)

Heaton Park boating lake, *c*. 1920.

Ornamental gardens from a postcard, *c.* 1908.

Visitors enjoying the grounds, with Heaton Hall in the background. This postcard probably dates from the turn of the century. (BLS)

Engraving of Heaton Hall, 1750, by an unknown artist. (BLS)

Heaton Hall in Edwardian times, from a glass negative. The Hall was designed by Wyatt. (BLS)

Staircase from Heaton Hall. It was used as a set in the television series *Brideshead Revisited*, which was screened in the early 1980s. (BLS)

Restored saloon, Heaton Hall. (BLS)

Chandelier from the Cupola Room. This room is
decorated in the rare Pompeiian style current
during the 1770s. (BLS)

The Dower House, Heaton Park. It has now so deteriorated through dry rot that only the façade remains. (BLS)

Heaton Park stables, *c.* 1908. (BLS)

A concert at Heaton Park on 1 July 1951. Many events have been staged in the grounds, from rock concerts to the visit of Pope John Paul II to Britain in 1982. (BLS)

Heaton Park Light Railway ran from the Grand Lodge to the Hall. Manchester Corporation operated it from 1924 to 1936, when it was dismantled on the grounds that it was uneconomical.

Kersal Moor, with a view of the old racecourse, 1930s. The hill on the left is Rainsough, and site of a Roman fort which would have overlooked the Irwell valley. Roman remains were also discovered at Prestwich Golf Course and traces of the old Roman road from Manchester to Ribchester lie adjacent to Bury New Road, which follows the Roman road's straight line.

BUILDINGS

Ivy Bank. This handsome house was situated on the corner of Bent Lane and Ostrich Lane.
Note the attractive buggy on the left.

Kersal Cell, where John Byrom composed the hymn 'Christians, awake'. Until its demolition, many locals held that it was haunted by the ghost of a monk.

Kersal Cell in happier times. Before it was knocked down, it was a public house and restaurant for many years. Perhaps the 'ghost' was a means of drumming up trade! (BLS)

Philips Park Hall, completed in 1830 for the Philips family, who resided there until the death of Anna Philips in 1946.

Philips Park lodge, also known locally as the 'Witch's Cottage'. This thatched cottage dates from the Regency period (1811–1820).

The 'Witch's Cottage' from a hand-coloured postcard. This building was demolished in 1969 to make way for the M62, after being fired by vandals and lying in a neglected condition for some time.

Butt Hill, built in 1778 for John Hope. The house takes its name from the village archery field; the targets, or 'butts', were still visible early this century. (BLS)

The fine gardens and pond at Butt Hill. (BLS)

The next three pictures beautifully illustrate the Victorian style of gracious living. They are all taken at Butt Hill. This is a view of the drawing room. (BLS)

Another view of the drawing room, Butt Hill. (BLS)

The dining room, Butt Hill. (BLS)

Southern's Cottage, *c*. 1900. This was an inn on the packhorse trail that crossed Bradley Ford at the Irwell. The trail came down Mere Clough, and over the river to Clifton.

The lodge house at Rainsough. Once the Rainsough tollhouse, it still stands – though its distinctive tall chimney has gone.

Bent Hill, 1990. Bent Hill, now an old people's home, was Prestwich Town Hall from 1920 to 1972, when the council amalgamated with Bury. (BLS)

The grounds of Drinkwater Park, *c.* 1900. Drinkwater Park surrounded Irwell House, which was home to the Drinkwaters from 1794. Through the 1794 purchase the Drinkwaters effectively owned the ancient manor of Prestwich. (BLS)

The ruins of Irwell House, 1967. It was fired in a civil defence exercise in 1958 after lying decayed and abandoned for many years. (BLS)

Cuckoo's Nest, 1967. The house was extended in 1830 by Roger Yates 'ut Neest', who ran his business as a manufacturer of handloom goods from this address. He walked to Manchester several times a week, and was 'never known to indulge in the luxury of Riding', according to contemporary sources. (BLS)

Kirkhams, 1990. This was once home of the family that gave this district of Prestwich its name. (BLS)

Rainsough workhouse, built in 1819. The site was occupied by the pub called The Staff of Life until recently. (BLS)

Bowman Street, 1967. The whole street was demolished soon after this photograph was taken, to make way for the present Housing Association development. (BLS)

The smallest house in Lancashire, 1967. This building was on Church Lane and was known locally as 'The Castle'. It still exists, though it has been amalgamated with the larger property next door.

The 'tin mission'. Temporary church buildings often preceded construction of more permanent ones. Another Prestwich example is St Hilda's iron church, built in 1887. The church is gone but St Hilda's Primary School stayed open until 1983.

St Margaret's church, early this century. Founded in 1849, it was enlarged and reopened during the Diamond Jubilee of Queen Victoria.

Catholic Church & Vicarage, Prestwich

Our Lady of Grace Catholic school, chapel, and presbytery, 1895. The Catholic church was built between these two buildings in 1931. The Catholic population in Prestwich was swelled by the recruitment of Irish nurses to work in Prestwich hospital during the latter part of the last century.

VILLAGE LIFE

Bury New Road, 1970s. Tower Buildings, built in 1926 as premises for Prestwich Co-op, is visible on the far left.

Prestwich village approached through Longfield, 1930s. The façade of the Grapes Inn, centre, is essentially unchanged to this day. Longfield was razed in 1965, but owing to a dispute with the builders, the site lay vacant for two years until the Longfield Centre was built in 1967.

Hilton Lane junction, 1940s.

The Petrocokino family. Thermistocles Petrocokino and his family lived at Sedgeley House between 1876 and 1900. At this time Prestwich was becoming increasingly popular with industrialists looking for a rural retreat within easy reach of Manchester. (BLS)

Benjamin Carver of Polefield House
(pictured also on page 4), *c.* 1900. A famous
benefactor in Prestwich and numerous local
documents attest to his presence at charity
events. He is pictured here in old age.

Local midwife, *c.* 1900. This lady's name was
probably Thorpe. It is interesting to speculate
how many villagers she helped to deliver into
the world. (BLS)

Mr Ford, a local character in Rainsough who took slides, such as this one, between 1924 and 1925. (BLS)

The Hanging Woods, near Drinkwater. The lodge and farm buildings are at the bottom of the valley.

A view from the top of Gardner Mount, also known as Spy-in-Cop, *c.* 1910. (BLS)

Waterdale near Drinkwater frozen over, *c.* 1895. (BLS)

Entrance to Drinkwater Park, with a lodge in the background, *c.* 1900.

These worthy gentlemen represent the Prestwich Bowls Club, *c.* 1880. (BLS)

A game of bowls at Prestwich Bowls Club. This picture was taken after the Second World War. (BLS)

A rare photograph of Simister. This shows Simister Lane, named after John Somister who owned a large farm in this area. 'Somister' became Simister, and still retains Prestwich's old rural character. (BLS)

PUBLIC HOUSES AND SHOPS

Farmer's Arms, Simister, c. 1920.

A performing bear outside the Staff of Life, Rainsough, early this century. Jimmy Heywood, the landlord, is on the right.

A group setting off on an outing, 1920s. This was taken outside the Staff of Life, Rainsough.

The Plough Inn having its sign repainted. Robert Edwards was the licensee, and beer was 5*d* a pint. The good old days, indeed.

A view of the Plough Inn and the Staff of Life on Rainsough Brow. The Staff of Life occupies the position of the old workhouse, and was built in 1819. Demolished in 1974, it was rebuilt on the same site. (BLS)

The old Friendship Tavern, Hope Square, 1890s. The original Friendship Tavern was built in 1847. In 1924 the new Friendship Inn was built in front of it, and Hope Square cottages and the old inn were knocked down. The new inn still stands.

County Wine Stores, Clarks Hill, 1960s. This picture predates the new housing that was to go up on the right. (BLS)

A very early picture of the County Wine Stores, *c.* 1905. The name Clarks Hill comes from the fact that the road ran through the meadow belonging to the parish clerk.

The Church Inn, 1960s. Once called the Ostrich Inn, the original building dates back to the seventeenth century. It was home to the infamous 'Star Chamber' where the Justice of the Peace held court. (BLS)

Original site of Ring o' Bells public house, 1972. This pub was on Church Lane, and was converted to the private residence shown above. (BLS)

The Ring o' Bells public house between 1904 and 1913, when Richard Dawson was landlord.

A mock 'hunting-party' in livery outside the Wilton Arms, 1920s. Despite recent name changes, this pub is still known locally as the Wilton.

The Forester's Arms, *c.* 1965. The façade has altered radically since. (BLS)

Heaton Park Bazaar, *c.* 1910. The diversity of goods on display reflects life before supermarkets and shopping centres became the norm.

The Ostrich, Bury Old Road. This pub is not very different now.

SCHOOL AND WORK

*Victorian school scene. This might be St Margaret's School, built in 1870 but used as an infant school since 1882.
St Margaret's School is situated off Bury Old Road, near Heaton Park. (BLS)*

Dressing up, perhaps for a parade or carnival. The school is unidentified. (BLS)

Seven dwarfs? These children would be great-grandfathers by now. Both these photographs are taken at the same unknown school. (BLS)

A children's party from the 1940s. One of these little mites is Mr Len Pennington, who lent many of the photographs that appear in this book. This photograph was taken in the Wesleyan Chapel, Rainsough.

A Coronation class photograph, 1937. These girls attended Hope Park School at the time of George VI and Queen Mary's Coronation.

Class Standard 2, Prestwich National School, *c.* 1928. The teachers are Mr Rigby and Miss Darragh. (BLS)

Hope Farm from a glass negative, *c.* 1907. The caption is reversed due to the photographer forgetting this would happen when the print was made. Clearly this was a prosperous farm, with neatly whitewashed walls and a natty buggy drawn up outside. (BLS)

Butt Hill Farm, from the farm survey of 1910. The family are stood outside, waiting rigidly for the photograph to be taken. District Health Commissions surveyed farms regularly to ensure that they were not overcrowded or unsanitary. A similar survey took place in 1898. (BLS)

Cambashaw Farm, from the 1910 farm survey. (BLS)

Diggle Fold barn, Lowther Road, 1967. It was demolished in 1969. (BLS)

Diggle Fold Farm, near Lowther Road. The Diggles were a Prestwich family of some antiquity, and the farm was in their hands from 1659 to 1810 – passing out of the family with the death of John Diggle.

Diggle Fold Farm, from the 1910 farm survey. (BLS)

High Bank Farm and all the family, including the dogs, from the 1910 farm survey. (BLS)

Drinkwater Park Farm, from the 1910 farm survey. (BLS)

Two boys play outside Drinkwater Park Farm, 1912. (BLS)

Dyers and finishers at Bleakleys, *c.* 1900. The factory was also known as the Myrtle Grove works. The Bleakley family ran the factory from 1819 until its sale to Messrs Whitehead at Elton in 1902. (BLS)

The old fire station, 1968. This is now a car park. The new fire station is on Bury New Road, and was built shortly after this picture was taken. (BLS)

Prestwich's first mail van, *c.* 1900. Before this date the postman was forbidden to leave the King's Highway, and post was left in shop windows for collection. Wealthy families made use of the Royal Mail coach on its journeys to Manchester. (BLS)

A farmer drives his sheep up Rainsough Brow, presumably for slaughter, *c.* 1910.

Sheep being driven into Harrison's, a butcher's shop with its own slaughterhouse, which was on the corner of Church Lane and Bury New Road. This picture was probably taken in about 1906.

Prestwich Hospital Lodge on Clifton Road. The hospital was first founded as Prestwich County Asylum in 1847. Until recently it was Prestwich's largest single employer.

Doctor's House, Prestwich Hospital, *c.* 1901. Most of these buildings have been or are being demolished to make way for the Tesco supermarket.

Superintendent's House, Prestwich Hospital, *c.* 1901.

Prestwich Hospital canteen, 1926. Both these photographs were lent by Mrs M. Cartwright, whose father-in-law is the gentleman in the apron. He worked at Prestwich Hospital for a while as a cooper.

A picket at Prestwich Hospital, 1982. The union NUPE is now amalgamated into UNISON. Throughout the eighties, the hospital was increasingly the victim of cuts and ward closures. It is now very much reduced in patient numbers and staff. Tesco now occupies a large part of its original land. (BLS)

Thomas Wrigley Ltd, 1950s. This was a civil engineering business that opened in Prestwich in 1916, and occupied one side of Prestwich station goods yard.

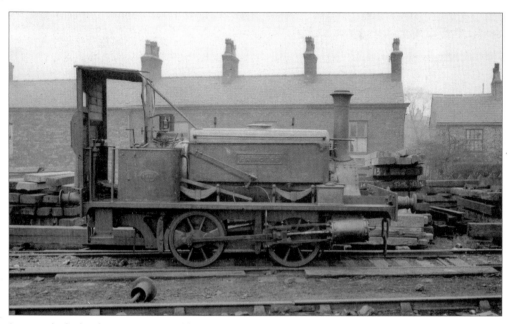

'Princess', the last locomotive owned by the Wrigleys. She was built in Leeds in 1897. Her last contract was at Irwell Park Wharf in 1946–7, and in 1953 she was scrapped.

EVENTS

Longfield day trip to Southport for the elderly, 1953. Leftover money made from whist drives to help the boys during the Second World War was used to pay for this expedition.

Longfield day trip, 1953. Left to right: Mrs Lucy Turner, the Mayor Mrs McVitie, Mr Halton, Mrs Jefferson, Mrs Royle, Mrs Jennings (née Sigsworth), Miss Sigsworth, Mr Bowden, Maggie Beard, Mrs Rose (née Strapps), Mr

Partington, Mrs Whitehead, Mrs Partington, Mrs Cunliffe, Mr Cunliffe, Mrs Halton, Mrs Bradshaw, Mrs Lucy Taylor, —?—, Mrs Walman, Mr Reece, Mr Barlow, and Mrs Hart. (BLS)

Besses-o'-th'-Barn band in full costume. The musicians in the original band fell out on the way home from playing at the Earl of Wilton's daughter's wedding in 1853; however, the band was revived and continues to this day. In its heyday it was considered the 'best band in the world', and toured as far afield as Australia. (BLS)

Massed choirs festival on the Heys, then called Grimshaws, June 1922. The Prestwich brass band is central. (BLS)

Local lads in the 20th SBM Regiment (5th Pals), at Morecambe. They were on their way to the battles of the First World War and many would not return. This photograph suffered considerable damage from damp before it was entrusted to Prestwich Library. (BLS)

These ladies, photographed in 1905, were the guests at a garden party given at Langley House for the members of St Margaret's Mothers' Union. The party was given by Miss Tomlin, who might very well be the severe lady in the centre front row, sitting in a wheelchair. (BLS)

The Jubilee year for St Margaret's School was 1910, and a ceremony was held to honour the occasion. A Miss Barlow is hoisting the flag, while assembled dignitaries look on. By 1902 the attendance at this school had gone from a single Sunday school class to 270 pupils.

PRESTWICH BOTANICAL SOCIETY'S GARDEN, OPENED SEPR 1913

The Prestwich Botanical Society, seen here in 1913, was established on 11 September 1820, at the Cock and Trumpet Inn, Rooden Lane. About twenty-five gentlemen met to discuss the subject, and the society had an extensive library and herbarium. By 1900 these meetings were taking place in the Railway and Naturalist public house, or 'the Nats', which is still open. The society was suspended during the First World War and not revived. (BLS)

Monument to the Pope's visit, unveiled by the Bishop of Salford, the Right Reverend Thomas Holland, in 1982. (BLS)

The gates at Beth David, where the Prestwich coin hoard was found in 1972. The gates are on Bury New Road, which is believed to follow the course of the old Roman road. The coins, mostly medieval, were found just beyond the gates. (BLS)

The Mayfair cinema, after being destroyed by fire in the 1950s. The Mayfair, now closed, was a replacement for the original Mayfair, which burnt down in about 1954, and was not rebuilt for a couple of years. (BLS)

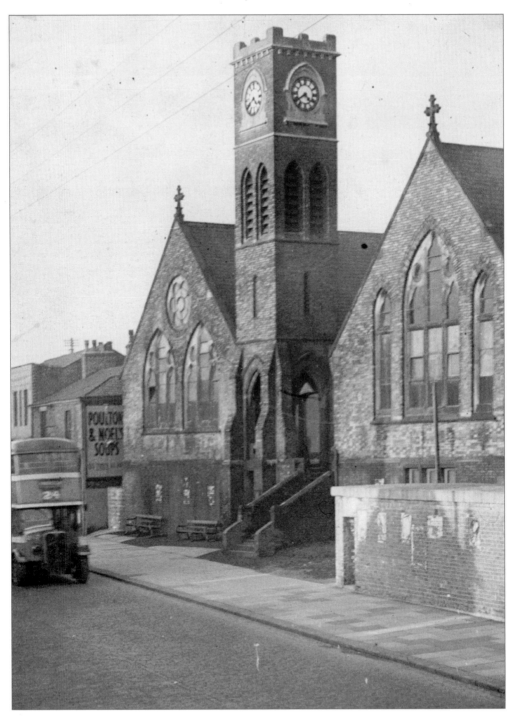

The National School, Prestwich, 1939. Note the air raid shelter in front of the building. Founded in 1817 and rebuilt in 1865, the National School operated until 1983, when it was demolished. (BLS)

Prestwich Autumn Horse Show, at Drinkwater, 28 September 1946. (BLS)

Agecroft Regatta, with Kersal Cell in the background, 27 June 1953. (BLS)

Agecroft Regatta on the River Irwell, 27 June 1953. Even then the river was polluted: it would be a bold move to row a tub on it, unless one was very sure of not capsizing! (BLS)

PROCESSIONS AND CARNIVALS

Sunday school walk, Church Lane, 1912. Whit walks and church 'wakes' were well-attended religious events. In the case of the wakes, there were also some rambunctious ones. Middleton describes the fighting and drinking common at a Wake, and villagers competed in a host of events, such as smoking matches and greasy pole-climbing.

Sunday school walk, Church Lane, 1912. These are doubtless St Mary's church walks.

Catholic walks, c. 1900. The building next to Smethursts may be the long-vanished Albion Inn on the corner of Church Lane. (BLS)

St Mary's church walk, taken before 1902 and the onset of electric trams. The two gentlemen at the front are probably Benjamin Carver of Polefield House and George Middleton, author of the *Annals of Prestwich* and enthusiastic local antiquarian.

Pre-1914 church procession along Bury New Road, with brass band preceding. Crowds line the street enthusiastically, much as they do today.

These beautifully turned-out little girls pause in a Whit walk for a photo opportunity, *c.* 1909.

Children dance with garlands during a Whit procession outside Bannisters shop, Bury New Road. Opposite was the Methodist chapel.

Urchins at Rainsough watching the procession go by, *c.* 1910. Many are in carnival costume.

Maypole dancers at Rainsough, *c.* 1910.

Church walkers bearing the Rainsough Wesleyan Sunday School banner, *c.* 1912. Rainsough Wesleyan Chapel, founded in 1874, was subject to the main church at Prestwich.

An early carnival float, drawn by a horse, at Rainsough. (BLS)

A beautiful day for the Prestwich Carnival, 23 June 1956. This is usually held on St Mary's Playing Fields, since they were drained and levelled in 1931. (BLS)

Prestwich Carnival, 23 June 1956. Local people dress up and contribute to the fun. (BLS)

MISCELLANY

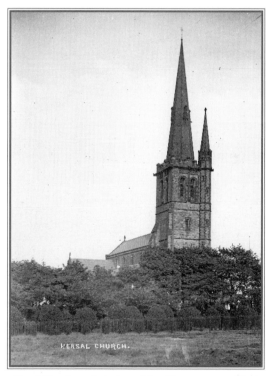

Kersal Church, with the line of the old racecourse visible in front.

Kersal Bar, site of the old tollgate, 1910. The little kiosk in the centre is still standing, although it is now abandoned and decayed.

Trams at Heaton Park station, *c.* 1903. These trams were run by the Salford Corporation. (BLS)

One of the original electric trains dating from 1916, when the Lancashire and Yorkshire Railway electrified the line from Manchester Victoria to Bury.

One of the original trains in Heaton Park station, 1956. The trains were replaced in 1959 by British Railways. In 1991 the lines were closed, to be reopened as the Metrolink tram service in 1992.

Kersal Bar. The tram is going to Eccles. The tram service, when it operated, was far more extensive than the present bus service. The tickets cost 2½d when the trams started running in 1902, 2d dearer than the figure preferred by Prestwich council.

The kiosk and sweet shop on Bury Old Road, 1971. This building was demolished in April 1973. (BLS)

A view of Sedgeley Park, Bury New Road, while the trams were in operation.

Sedgeley Park, Bury New Road, 1930s. Note the handsome period car on the right.

Steam lorry, Bury New Road, 1940s. Built in 1918, this Sentinel lorry ran from Bury to Manchester and back each day, the last steam lorry to travel through Prestwich regularly. It is now preserved and shown in road steam rallies.

The Manchester to Bury Horse Bus, 1890. Before trams, the main means of public transport between Manchester and Prestwich were the horse bus and the Manchester to Bury railway line, built in the 1870s. The route of this railway line is now used by Metrolink. (BLS)

The first Salford Electric Cars to Prestwich, 5 April 1902. The tram opening is attended by the Mayor and various local worthies, all male. The splendidly decorated tram is waiting outside Chester Bank, home of the Town Hall offices until 1920. The trams stopped running in 1935/6. (BLS)

Prestwich Bowls Club, after 1915. The membership had expanded considerably since the earlier picture was taken (page 65). The old bowling green is now gone, but bowls is now played in St Mary's gardens, behind Prestwich Conservative Club. (BLS)

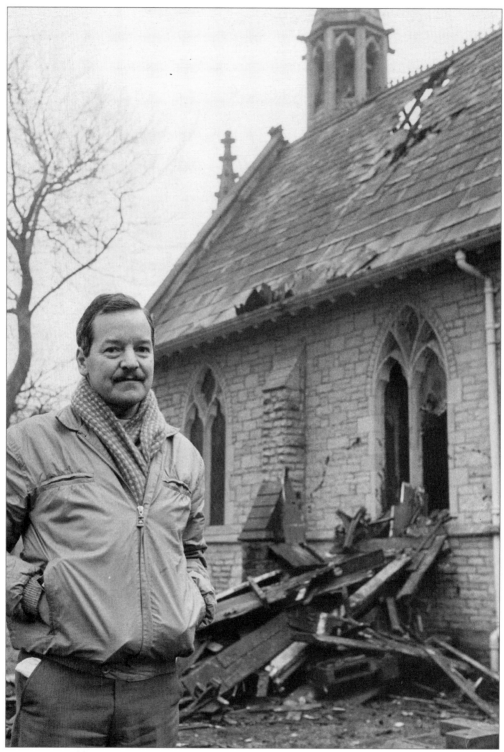

St Margaret's church after it was devastated by fire, 21 February 1985. The fire, believed to be the work of an arsonist, caused £20,000 worth of damage. The man is unidentified. (BLS)

The interior of St Margaret's church after the fire, 21 February 1985. (BLS)

The building of the M62 in 1969 caused many local changes. Philips Park Lodge, or the 'Witch's Cottage', was demolished to make way for it, and the motorway effectively cut Prestwich off from Whitefield. It was the nearness of the motorway which doubtless encouraged the developers of the new shopping centre to continue with their plans despite the strong objections of local people. Though Prestwich has become progressively less rural from the beginning of this century, the new motorway hastened the process of urbanization.

'Convict 99'. This mysterious picture, from the archives at Prestwich Library, remains an enigma. Perhaps it has some connection with Prestwich Hospital, which even today houses some prisoners before trial. The author would greatly welcome any information regarding this unusual photograph.(BLS)

ACKNOWLEDGEMENTS

This book would have been impossible without the very generous and patient assistance rendered to me by the following people. Wherever the book succeeds, it is due entirely to them; where it falls down, there is nobody to blame but me.

I would firstly like to thank Bury Library Services (BLS), who contributed the majority of photographs to this book, and who were helpful and obliging throughout. I would also like to thank Len Pennington, who very generously let me sift through the best photographs in his staggering collection, and who indulged me endlessly in my very vague requests for background information on the pictures. Thanks are also due to Alex Appleton, both for his photographs and his exhaustive knowledge of transport history, amongst other things. I would also like to thank Mrs M. Cartwright, who contributed photographs of the interior of Prestwich Hospital, long after I had despaired of ever finding such pictures.

For support and occasional pints bought me during times of crisis, I must thank the staff at Dillons, Manchester, especially Lesley Baker. Many thanks must go to my editor at Sutton Publishing, Simon Fletcher, for guiding me through the minefield of local history publishing. And, finally, my greatest thanks must go to my friends Julie Revell, Marcelle Lipman, and my parents, George and Ellen Callaghan, who encouraged and supported me throughout everything.

BRITAIN IN OLD PHOTOGRAPHS

Lincoln
Lincoln Cathedral
The Lincolnshire Coast
Liverpool
Around Llandudno
Around Lochaber
Theatrical London
Around Louth
The Lower Fal Estuary
Lowestoft
Luton
Lympne Airfield
Lytham St Annes
Maidenhead
Around Maidenhead
Around Malvern
Manchester
Manchester Road & Rail
Mansfield
Marlborough: A Second Selection
Marylebone & Paddington
Around Matlock
Melton Mowbray
Around Melksham
The Mendips
Merton & Morden
Middlesbrough
Midsomer Norton & Radstock
Around Mildenhall
Milton Keynes
Minehead
Monmouth & the River Wye
The Nadder Valley
Newark
Around Newark
Newbury
Newport, Isle of Wight
The Norfolk Broads
Norfolk at War
North Fylde
North Lambeth
North Walsham & District
Northallerton
Northampton
Around Norwich
Nottingham 1944–74
The Changing Face of Nottingham
Victorian Nottingham
Nottingham Yesterday & Today
Nuneaton
Around Oakham
Ormskirk & District
Otley & District
Oxford: The University
Oxford Yesterday & Today
Oxfordshire Railways: A Second
  Selection
Oxfordshire at School
Around Padstow
Pattingham & Wombourne

Penwith
Penzance & Newlyn
Around Pershore
Around Plymouth
Poole
Portsmouth
Poulton-le-Fylde
Preston
Prestwich
Pudsey
Radcliffe
RAF Chivenor
RAF Cosford
RAF Hawkinge
RAF Manston
RAF Manston: A Second Selection
RAF St Mawgan
RAF Tangmere
Ramsgate & Thanet Life
Reading
Reading: A Second Selection
Redditch & the Needle District
Redditch: A Second Selection
Richmond, Surrey
Rickmansworth
Around Ripley
The River Soar
Romney Marsh
Romney Marsh: A Second
  Selection
Rossendale
Around Rotherham
Rugby
Around Rugeley
Ruislip
St Albans
St Andrews
Salford
Salisbury
Salisbury: A Second Selection
Salisbury: A Third Selection
Around Salisbury
Sandhurst & Crowthorne
Sandown & Shanklin
Sandwich
Scarborough
Scunthorpe
Seaton, Lyme Regis & Axminster
Around Seaton & Sidmouth
Sedgley & District
The Severn Vale
Sherwood Forest
Shrewsbury
Shrewsbury: A Second Selection
Shropshire Railways
Skegness
Around Skegness
Skipton & the Dales
Around Slough

Smethwick
Somerton & Langport
Southampton
Southend-on-Sea
Southport
Southwark
Southwell
Southwold to Aldeburgh
Stafford
Around Stafford
Staffordshire Railways
Around Staveley
Stepney
Stevenage
The History of Stilton Cheese
Stoke-on-Trent
Stoke Newington
Stonehouse to Painswick
Around Stony Stratford
Around Stony Stratford: A Second
  Selection
Stowmarket
Streatham
Stroud & the Five Valleys
Stroud & the Five Valleys: A
  Second Selection
Stroud's Golden Valley
The Stroudwater and Thames &
  Severn Canals
The Stroudwater and Thames &
  Severn Canals: A Second
  Selection
Suffolk at Work
Suffolk at Work: A Second
  Selection
The Heart of Suffolk
Sunderland
Sutton
Swansea
Swindon: A Third Selection
Swindon: A Fifth Selection
Around Tamworth
Taunton
Around Taunton
Teesdale
Teesdale: A Second Selection
Tenbury Wells
Around Tettenhall & Codshall
Tewkesbury & the Vale of
  Gloucester
Thame to Watlington
Around Thatcham
Around Thirsk
Thornbury to Berkeley
Tipton
Around Tonbridge
Trowbridge
Around Truro
TT Races
Tunbridge Wells

Tunbridge Wells: A Second
  Selection
Twickenham
Uley, Dursley & Cam
The Upper Fal
The Upper Tywi Valley
Uxbridge, Hillingdon & Cowley
The Vale of Belvoir
The Vale of Conway
Ventnor
Wakefield
Wallingford
Walsall
Waltham Abbey
Wandsworth at War
Wantage, Faringdon & the Vale
  Villages
Around Warwick
Weardale
Weardale: A Second Selection
Wednesbury
Wells
Welshpool
West Bromwich
West Wight
Weston-super-Mare
Around Weston-super-Mare
Weymouth & Portland
Around Wheatley
Around Whetstone
Whitchurch to Market Drayton
Around Whitstable
Wigton & the Solway Plain
Willesden
Around Wilton
Wimbledon
Around Windsor
Wingham, Addisham &
  Littlebourne
Wisbech
Witham & District
Witney
Around Witney
The Witney District
Wokingham
Around Woodbridge
Around Woodstock
Woolwich
Woolwich Royal Arsenal
Around Wootton Bassett,
  Cricklade & Purton
Worcester
Worcester in a Day
Around Worcester
Worcestershire at Work
Around Worthing
Wotton-under-Edge to Chipping
  Sodbury
Wymondham & Attleborough
The Yorkshire Wolds

To order any of these titles please telephone our distributor, Littlehampton Book Services on 01903 721596
For a catalogue of these and our other titles please ring Regina Schinner on 01453 731114